GEOGRAPHY MATTERS IN
ANCIENT EGYPT

Melanie Waldron

heinemann
raintree

To contact Capstone Global Library, please call 800-747-4992, or visit our web site www.capstonepub.com

Edited by Helen Cox Cannons and Jennifer Besel
Designed by Philippa Jenkins
Original illustrations © Capstone Global Library Limited 2015
Illustrated by HL Studios, Witney, Oxon
Picture research by Jo Miller and Pam Mitsakos
Production by Helen McCreath
Originated by Capstone Global Library Ltd
Printed and bound in China by CTPS

18 17 16 15 14
10 9 8 7 6 5 4 3 2 1

Library of Congress Cataloging-in-Publication Data
Waldron, Melanie, author.
  Geography matters in ancient Egypt / Melanie Waldron.
     pages cm.—(Geography matters in ancient civilizations)
  Includes bibliographical references and index.
  ISBN 978-1-4846-0962-0 (hb)—ISBN 978-1-4846-0967-5 (pb)—ISBN 978-1-4846-0977-4 (ebook) 1. Egypt—Historical geography—Juvenile literature. 2. Human geography—Egypt—Juvenile literature. 3. Egypt—Civilization—To 332 B.C.—Juvenile literature. I. Title. II. Series: Geography matters in ancient civilizations.
  DT49.9.W35 2015
  932.01—dc23   2014013377

This book has been officially leveled by using the F&P Text Level Gradient™ Leveling System.

Acknowledgments
We would like to thank the following for permission to reproduce photographs: Alamy: © Ivan Vdovin, 9, © Maximilian Weinzierl, 12, © PRISMA ARCHIVO, 11, © NASA Archive, 7, © World History Archive, 20; AP Images: AP-Photo, 40; Corbis: © Chris Hellier, 15, © Werner Forman,23, 29; Dreamstime: © Sharifphoto, cover; Getty Images: Universal Images Group/Werner Forman, 39, De Agostini/DEA/A. GAROZZO, 14, De Agostini/DEA/G. LOVERA, 25, 36, Getty Images News/Patrick Landmann, 31, De Agostini/DEA/G. DAGLI ORTI, 33; Shutterstock: AridOcean, relief map (throughout), BasPhoto, 34,Chu Ching, 41, leoks, 16, N Mrtgh, 8, Nestor Noci, 6, Oleg Kozlov, 22, Fedor Selivanov, 37; Superstock:DeAgostini,18, 21, Iberfoto,19, Robert Harding Picture Library,38, Universal Images Group, 21. Design Elements: Nova Development Corporation, clip art (throughout).

We would like to thank Brian Williams for his invaluable help in the preparation of this book.

Every effort has been made to contact copyright holders of material reproduced in this book. Any omissions will be rectified in subsequent printings if notice is given to the publisher.

Contents

Some words are shown in bold, **like this**. You can find out what they mean by looking in the glossary.

Who Were the Ancient Egyptians?

The **civilization** of ancient Egypt lasted for about 3,000 years, from around 3100 BCE until 30 BCE. A civilization is an organized society with rules and customs. We know a lot about ancient Egyptian life from objects that **archaeologists** have found. These include **mummies**, treasure, and amazing buildings such as pyramids, temples, and **obelisks**. All of these finds have survived for thousands of years in the Egyptian landscape.

How did the civilization begin?

Before 3100 BCE, small groups of people lived in the area of ancient Egypt. Around 5500 BCE, some groups began to build small **settlements** near the Nile River. They started growing food in the river valley. The villages were grouped into two kingdoms: Upper Egypt and Lower Egypt. In 3100 BCE, these two kingdoms joined together, and this was the start of the ancient Egyptian civilization.

How was ancient Egyptian society organized?

The **pharaoh** was at the top of society. He was the king, and Egyptians believed he was a living god. The pharaoh had a team of important men to organize parts of society, such as the army, religion, and law. At the bottom of society were poor farmers, who worked on the land, and slaves. Slaves were not paid for their work.

DID YOU KNOW?
Ancient Egypt's picture writing remained a puzzle for hundreds of years. Then, in 1799, a Frenchman found a slab of rock at a place called Rosetta. This slab was covered in writing that helped people to understand the writing on some buildings. This sparked a lot of interest in ancient Egypt, and many adventurers came to the area looking for new discoveries.

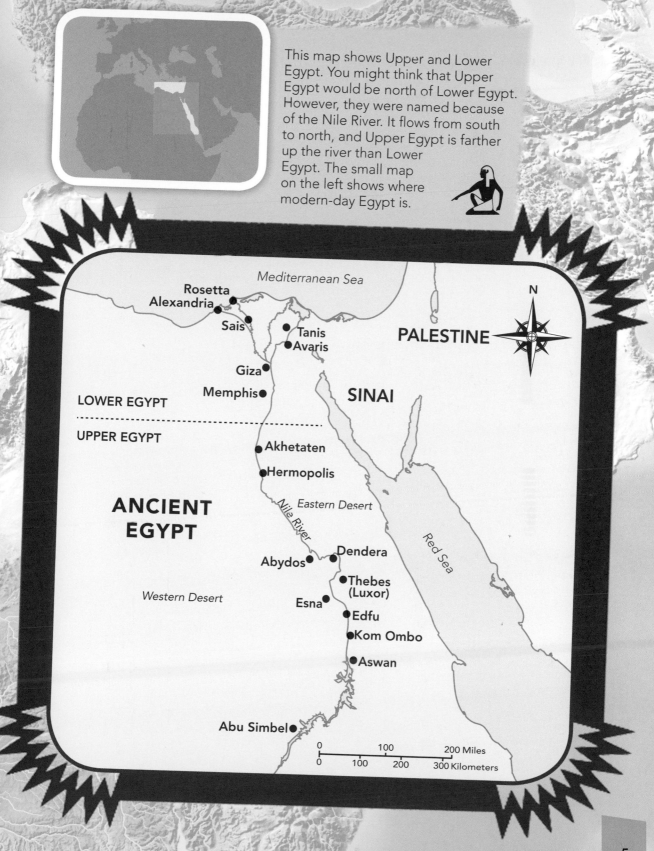

This map shows Upper and Lower Egypt. You might think that Upper Egypt would be north of Lower Egypt. However, they were named because of the Nile River. It flows from south to north, and Upper Egypt is farther up the river than Lower Egypt. The small map on the left shows where modern-day Egypt is.

Mediterranean Sea

N

Rosetta
Alexandria
Sais
Tanis
Avaris
PALESTINE
Giza
Memphis
SINAI

LOWER EGYPT

UPPER EGYPT

Akhetaten
Hermopolis

ANCIENT
EGYPT

Nile River
Eastern Desert

Abydos
Dendera
Thebes
(Luxor)
Red Sea
Esna
Edfu
Kom Ombo
Aswan

Western Desert

Abu Simbel

0   100   200 Miles
0   100   200   300 Kilometers

What were the ancient Egyptian kingdoms?

Although the civilization lasted for over 3,000 years, there were periods when it was weak and did not have strong leaders. Aside from these times, there were three main periods, or kingdoms, when the civilization was strong and powerful:

- Old Kingdom (2686 BCE to 2181 BCE): The Egyptians built huge pyramids at Giza. The pyramids were **tombs** for the pharaohs.
- Middle Kingdom (2055 BCE to 1650 BCE): The Egyptians took control of land to the south and so were able to farm more land.
- New Kingdom (1550 BCE to 1069 BCE): During this time, the area controlled by Egypt grew to its largest size.

After the end of the New Kingdom, other civilizations invaded Egypt. Finally, in 30 BCE, Egypt became part of the Roman **Empire**.

During the New Kingdom, pharaohs were buried in magnificent rock tombs in the Valley of the Kings, near the city of Thebes.

THE MIGHTY NILE

The area around the Nile River is called the Nile Basin, and it forms part of 10 African countries. The Nile Basin is over 1.3 million square miles (3.3 million square kilometers) in size, and 238 million people live there.

This image shows the Nile River from space. You can see settlements all along its length.

How did geography affect life in ancient Egypt?

People could not live in the desert, so they lived near the Nile River. Much of daily life depended on the river, as a **source** of water, for transportation, and for farming. Few people were as affected by the geography of their land as the ancient Egyptians.

7

Where in the World Was Ancient Egypt?

Egypt is in the northeastern part of Africa, where the **continent** meets Europe and Asia. Egypt has large areas of **barren** desert, with huge expanses of sand and sand dunes. The ancient Egyptians called the desert areas to the west of the Nile River the "red land." This land separated the civilization from others in Africa and pushed Egyptians to living near the Nile River, where they could get water and grow food. The "red land" made up about 90 percent of the area of ancient Egypt.

Egyptians could not live in the hot, dry desert areas. There was no water and no way to grow food.

DID YOU KNOW?

The climate of Egypt today is much the same as it was in ancient Egyptian times. It is hot and dry, and it hardly ever rains. In the north, the average daily temperature is about 68 degrees Fahrenheit (20 degrees Celsius), and in the south, the average is about 79 degrees Fahrenheit (26 degrees Celsius). The water in the Nile River flows from lands farther south that receive more rainfall.

This is one of the cataracts on the Nile River. The rocks make it difficult for boats to sail along the river.

How did the Nile River separate ancient Egypt from people farther south?

From its source in the middle of Africa, the Nile flows down some waterfalls and rock **rapids**. These are called **cataracts**. In ancient Egypt, there was a huge cataract at a place called Elephantine (now called Aswan). This cataract was very difficult to sail through, so it gave Egyptians protection from invaders from the south.

What were ancient Egypt's borders?

There are huge areas of desert to the west, south, and east of Egypt. The Red Sea beyond the eastern desert separates Egypt and Arabia (now Saudi Arabia). It runs up almost all of the eastern side of Egypt. To the north of the country is the Mediterranean Sea.

This geography means that ancient Egypt's only land bridge to other civilizations was the narrow strip of land in the northeastern corner of the country. This was Egypt's link to the Sinai **Peninsula** and other empires in Asia, such as those of Persia (now Iran) and Mesopotamia (now eastern Syria, southeast Turkey, and most of Iraq).

How was ancient Egypt's culture affected by its location?

At first, the Egyptians kept to themselves, developing a society and **culture** of their own. For example, they developed their own system of writing, their own religion, and their own style of art. Desert and water were key features of geography that kept the Egyptians separated from other peoples. Deserts and oceans were difficult to cross, and the cataracts in the Nile stopped enemies from attacking from the south. The Egyptians felt safe, and therefore they had only small armies.

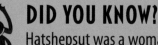

DID YOU KNOW?

Hatshepsut was a woman who became one of ancient Egypt's kings. She even dressed like a male pharaoh, sometimes wearing a fake beard, as male kings did! She was a strong leader and defended Egypt's borders against attacks from other civilizations.

This wall painting in a temple shows Egyptian soldiers marching on an expedition.

However, as the kingdoms grew, the Egyptians began mixing with other empires and civilizations. They traded with them and sometimes went to war with them. Toward the end of ancient Egypt, many different foreign powers had invaded and brought their own cultures to mix with that of the Egyptians.

How Did the Nile River Shape Ancient Egyptian Life?

The Nile River is the longest river in the world. It is 4,132 miles (6,650 kilometers) long, and it starts far to the south of Egypt. Most of ancient Egypt was dry desert. From the very beginning, the civilization grew up on the banks of the river, as far as the Nile **Delta**.

This picture shows how the land along the banks of the Nile River is lush and fertile today, compared with the dry, barren desert of the rest of Egypt.

What is the Nile Delta?

The Nile River flows into the Mediterranean Sea in north Egypt. Around 93 miles (150 kilometers) before it reaches the coast, the river valley spreads out into a large fan shape called a delta. The delta is about 155 miles (250 kilometers) wide at the coast. Many settlements grew up in the **fertile** land in the delta.

In ancient Egyptian times, the Nile River split into about seven channels when it reached the delta. This happened because the river began to flow more slowly over the flatter land near the coast, and it dropped many of the tiny particles of mud and **silt** that it had carried on its journey. Over time, this created mud banks that the river had to weave around in smaller channels.

Why were the yearly floods so important?

The Nile River flooded every year, from about June until October or November. Rain and melted snow from the mountains far to the south of Egypt would drain into the river.

When the river flooded the land, it left behind tiny particles of silt. The silt contained **minerals** that made the soil fertile. Crops grew well in the mineral-rich soil.

This map of the Nile River shows the area of land that was flooded each year. Egyptians called this the "black land," from the mineral-rich silt that helped crops to grow.

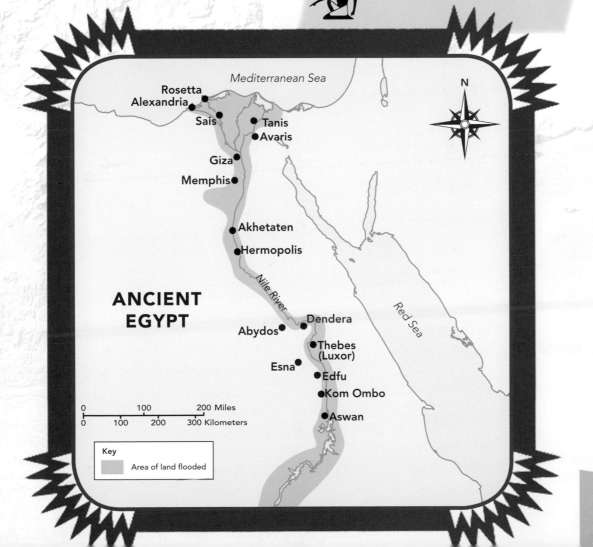

Mediterranean Sea

N

Rosetta
Alexandria
Sais
Tanis
Avaris
Giza
Memphis
Akhetaten
Hermopolis
Nile River
Red Sea

ANCIENT EGYPT

Dendera
Abydos
Thebes (Luxor)
Esna
Edfu
Kom Ombo
Aswan

0   100   200 Miles
0   100   200   300 Kilometers

Key
Area of land flooded

Did the floods happen every year?

In normal conditions, the Nile River flooded at the same time every year. In a year with too much flooding, villages could be washed away and fields could be destroyed. If there was too little flooding, the soil would not get the minerals it needed. This led to poor harvests and **famine**.

How did ancient Egyptians use the water from the Nile River?

The Nile River was essential for life in ancient Egypt. Egyptians used water for **irrigation**, to water crops. They also used it as drinking water for themselves and for animals. When the river was not flooding, Egyptians dug channels in the riverbanks. These were used to move water away from the river. The channels would feed into large ponds that acted as **reservoirs**. These ponds would hold enough water to supply towns and farmers when the river levels were low.

THE NILOMETER

Egyptians built measuring devices called Nilometers along the river. These helped them to check the level of flooding. Stepped Nilometers were like staircases leading down to the river. Each step was covered in turn as the water level rose.

What was a shaduf?

In the New Kingdom, a machine called a **shaduf** was invented. It had a bucket on one end of a long pole with a weight attached to the other end. The pole rested on a wooden frame. When the weighted end was lifted up, the bucket end dropped into the water and scooped some up. Then the weighted end dropped so that the bucket lifted up. The pole could then swing to the side, and the water was poured out of the bucket and into a channel.

A shaduf could lift water up from the river and feed it into the channels and ponds, even when the river levels were low.

How did the ancient Egyptians use the Nile River for transportation?

The Nile River, and the canals that people dug in the river valley, were very important for transportation in ancient Egypt. There were very few roads, since most people only traveled short distances on land. People used boats to travel longer distances and to cross the river.

The ancient Egyptians added sails to their riverboats, which helped to move the boats along when it was windy.

DID YOU KNOW?
Some barges were so big they could carry whole stone pillars called obelisks. Historians think that the female pharaoh Hatshepsut had huge obelisks transported on barges that were over 260 feet (80 meters) long!

Boats and ships carried people visiting friends or relatives as well as traders traveling to markets. Some boats carried cargo such as food; others carried huge blocks of stone for building great temples, tombs, and palaces. After death, the bodies of wealthy people were transported by funeral barges.

What were the rivercraft made of?

People used simple rafts for fishing and hunting on the river. These were made of **papyrus** reeds, and people used paddles to steer and propel them. Larger boats were made from wood. However, there were very few large trees in Egypt, so the wood had to be **imported** from other countries.

Some of the huge barges on the river were too heavy to row. They were towed by lots of smaller boats powered by teams of rowers with oars. Some of the larger barges were towed by as many as 27 boats.

How Did Ancient Egyptians Farm the Land?

The fertile soils created by the floods meant that farming was a large part of Egyptian life. People believed that all the land belonged to the gods, and so the pharaoh was the living owner of all the land. He shared some of it with wealthy people or temples. However, most villagers worked on the land for the landowners.

When did the farming year begin?

The farming year began when the floodwaters dropped in late October or November. Farmers started plowing the soil and sowing seeds. They had to work quickly because the heat of the sun would soon bake the ground hard and make it difficult to work.

The land was plowed using simple plows pulled behind one or two oxen. The seeds were scattered by hand and then trampled into the ground by sheep or goats.

DID YOU KNOW?

Some ancient Egyptian farmers trained monkeys to help them during harvest time. The monkeys would climb apple and pomegranate trees. They would pick the fruit, then carry it down to the farmers.

When did ancient Egyptians harvest the land?

Farmers harvested their crops between March and June. Farmers had to get their crops harvested as early as possible. This would allow time for a second batch of crops to be planted and harvested, and for irrigation channels to be repaired, before the next flood began.

This wall painting shows farmers winnowing their grain. They did this to separate the grain from the pieces of straw and chaff that were mixed with it. Winnowing was best done on a windy day, when the wind would blow away the light straw and chaff, leaving only the grain to fall to the ground.

What crops did ancient Egyptians grow?

Grains such as wheat and barley were important crops. Egyptians grew these as their first crops. They used them to make bread, porridge, and beer. After farmers harvested the grain, they planted their second crops, such as beans, onions, and melons. They also grew grapes, figs, and dates, as well as flax that was used to make linen for clothing. A river plant called papyrus was another important crop. It was used to make shoes, boats, baskets, and papyrus paper.

This is a model of bakers making bread from the wheat grown on the land. It was found in an Egyptian tomb.

PAPER FROM PLANTS

Papyrus plants were used to make papyrus paper. The tough outer skin of the stem was removed and the inner part was cut into thin strips. After these strips had been soaked in water, they were arranged into sheets, with their edges overlapping. After they had been weighted down and left to dry, they were used as **scrolls** of paper (called papyrus). Only highly educated people called **scribes** used this precious material.

What animals did ancient Egyptians farm?

Egyptians raised cows, sheep, and goats. They used the meat and milk from the animals, and they made clothes and sandals out of their skins. They also raised birds like ducks and geese and ate their eggs and meat. However, only wealthy people ate meat often. Fish such as perch, catfish, and tilapia would be caught directly from the Nile River and would also be reared in fishponds. Egyptians used honey to sweeten their food.

This wall painting shows an Egyptian woman fishing and hunting in marshland.

HUNTING BIRDS

Ancient Egyptians took advantage of the flooding of the Nile River in other ways. The floodwaters attracted many different birds to the area. Farmers would trap these for food, but others hunted them for fun.

What did farmers do during the weeks of flooding?

When the Nile River flooded, the farmland was covered with water. During this time, farmers would mend their farming tools. Since the tools were made from wood, they were easily worn out and broken. Farmers also looked after their animals. Sometimes the farmers were called upon to help in building projects for the pharaoh.

Farmers would check the level of flooding and build up **embankments** along the edges of channels, if the flood levels were high. This would control the flow of water in the channels and would also protect villages and other buildings. Even buildings built on slightly higher ground were at risk if the floods were high.

Embankments protect some areas from flooding today, just as in ancient Egyptian times.

FARMING TOOLS

Most ancient Egyptian farming tools were made of wood. Wooden hoes were used to break up soil. Sickles had wooden handles and sharp blades made of a type of stone called flint. Egyptians used these to harvest the wheat and barley. Farming in ancient Egypt was very hard work compared to modern farming with machines!

This image shows rope-stretchers doing a crop survey. They were supervised by a scribe named Djerserkereseneb, and this image is on the wall of his tomb.

Why was the land surveyed each year?

After each flood, the markers that set out the area of each farmer's land had to be replaced. This is because they could be moved by the floodwater. The land had to be **surveyed** each year to make sure that each farmer was farming the correct area of land. Some Egyptians developed excellent land-surveying skills.

23

How Did the Ancient Egyptian Empire Change?

The geographical area of ancient Egypt did not change much during the Old Kingdom. In the Middle Kingdom, Egyptian power expanded to the south, into an area called Nubia. The Egyptians pushed their kingdom about 200 miles (320 kilometers) in this direction. Nubia became part of ancient Egypt, and the Egyptians built strong forts and temples.

This map shows the area of Nubia that Egyptian kings ruled over in the Middle Kingdom. It also shows where the Hyksos invaded from, and their capital, Avaris.

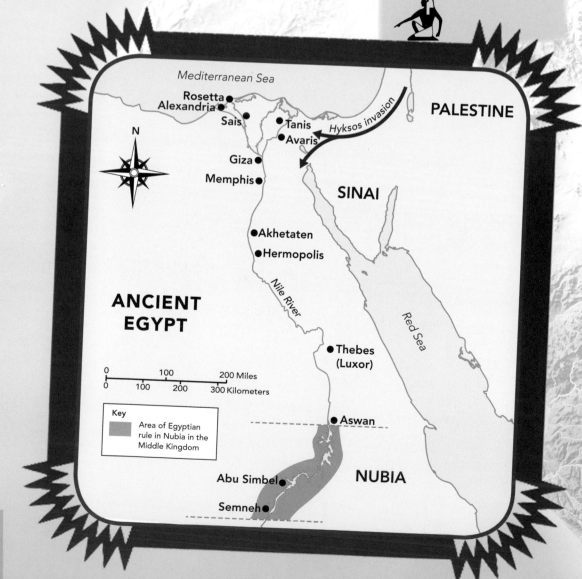

Mediterranean Sea

Rosetta
Alexandria
Sais
Tanis
Avaris
Hyksos invasion
PALESTINE

N

Giza
Memphis

SINAI

Akhetaten
Hermopolis

Nile River

ANCIENT
EGYPT

Red Sea

Thebes
(Luxor)

0   100   200 Miles
0   100   200   300 Kilometers

Key
Area of Egyptian rule in Nubia in the Middle Kingdom

Aswan

NUBIA

Abu Simbel
Semneh

The Hyksos brought the idea of chariots to the Egyptians.

What happened at the end of the Middle Kingdom?

Toward the end of the Middle Kingdom, the pharaohs became weak. People from lands east of Egypt started moving into the Nile Delta. Egyptians called these people Hyksos. They had a big impact on ancient Egyptian life, and their power grew. Eventually, they ruled over most of Egypt from their capital city of Avaris, in the Nile Delta.

How did the ancient Egyptians end Hyksos rule?

During the time of Hyksos rule, there were still Egyptian kings and princes living farther south of Avaris, in Thebes. They did not like the Hyksos ruling over Egypt. When they had grown powerful enough, they started to fight back. Eventually, they defeated the Hyksos in 1567 BCE. The Hyksos retreated to Palestine.

DID YOU KNOW?

The period of Hyksos rule actually helped the Egyptians. They started looking outward from their isolated geographical location and began to realize that they had to go into other countries to gain power and resources. They began to use techniques and ideas that the Hyksos had brought to Egypt.

What happened after the Hyksos were defeated?

After 1550 BCE, Egyptian rule grew strong again, and the New Kingdom began. Egyptian traders and soldiers traveled to places in Africa, Asia, and around the Mediterranean Sea. The Egyptian empire grew to its biggest size, ranging from Nubia in the south to Syria in the north.

N

Mediterranean Sea

Nile Delta

PALESTINE

SINAI

EGYPT

Nile River

Red Sea

NUBIA

0   100   200 Miles
0   100   200   300 Kilometers

Key

Largest size of Egyptian empire

This map shows the ancient Egyptian empire at its largest, during the New Kingdom.

A BOY KING

Tutankhamun was a pharaoh who ruled between 1336 and 1327 BCE. He was only nine years old when he became the pharaoh! He is famous because when his tomb was discovered in the Valley of the Kings in 1922, archaeologists found an amazing wealth of treasures buried with his mummy.

Although they gained a lot of wealth from their new lands, the Egyptians' main concern was keeping Egypt safe from attack by neighboring countries. The Nile cataracts, the deserts, the Red Sea, and the Mediterranean Sea helped to protect Egypt, but the Egyptians still had to protect themselves from invaders.

This headrest was found among the treasures in Tutankhamun's tomb. It is made of ivory.

What goods did the ancient Egyptians trade with other countries?

During years of low flooding, when crops failed, Egyptians had to trade with other countries to get grain. Goods such as wine, linen, papyrus, and gold were **exported** out of Egypt, as well as grain in good years. Egyptians imported goods such as oils, resin, silver, copper, horses, spices, and wood.

What Part Did the Desert Play in Ancient Egyptian Life?

Although much of ancient Egyptian life took place in the Nile Valley, the vast expanses of desert "red land" had valuable resources. However, there were no permanent settlements deep into the desert, since it would have been impossible to live there with no water.

This map shows the locations of some of the quarries and mines in ancient Egypt. Most of them are in the strip of desert between the Nile River and the Red Sea.

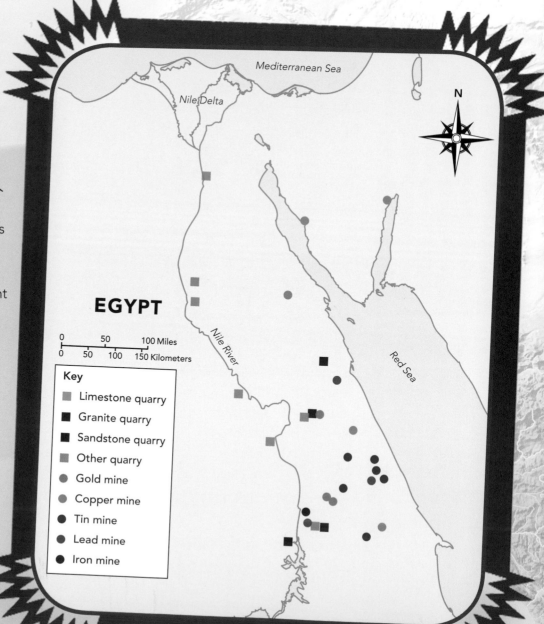

Mediterranean Sea

Nile Delta

N

EGYPT

0   50   100 Miles
0   50   100   150 Kilometers

Nile River

Red Sea

Key
- Limestone quarry
- Granite quarry
- Sandstone quarry
- Other quarry
- Gold mine
- Copper mine
- Tin mine
- Lead mine
- Iron mine

HARD STONE, SOFT STONE

Stone quarries were usually worked by slaves, who had the hard job of cutting, transporting, and shaping the stone blocks. Granite was the hardest rock that was quarried, and so it was usually used only in small blocks and for very special monuments. Limestone and sandstone were much easier to quarry, so these made up the bulk of the building blocks.

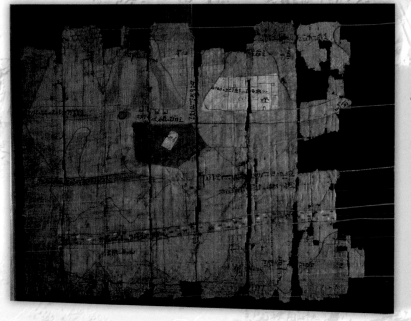

This delicate papyrus, from around 1150 BCE, is a map of the desert east of the Nile River. Historians think it is the world's earliest example of a map that shows different types of rock.

What resources did the desert provide?

Egyptians used resources that they could find in desert areas. They mined for gold and other metals, gemstones, and salts. They also mined huge blocks of different types of stone, including sandstone, limestone, basalt, and granite. They used this stone for buildings such as pyramids and temples.

Mineral salts were important, and not just for flavoring food. Egyptians used them to turn animal skins into leather, in medicine, and in making ceramics and glass. Salts were also used to **preserve** meat and in the process of mummification.

How did the ancient Egyptians make use of desert oases?

Oases are places in the desert where water that is normally held below ground level can come to the surface. This can happen if the land surface dips down, or if there is a natural spring that emerges at the surface.

Egyptians used oases in the desert as stopping points along trade routes to the west. Some oases gave refuge to people banished by Egyptian rulers. At Bahariya Oasis, Egyptians made wine, and archaeologists have discovered a huge collection of graves there, now called the Valley of the Golden Mummies. There is a temple to the god Amun at Dakhla Oasis, and Farafra Oasis had lush grasslands that were used to graze cattle.

This map shows oases in the desert west of the Nile River. In ancient Egypt, people managed to live around oases because they provided water.

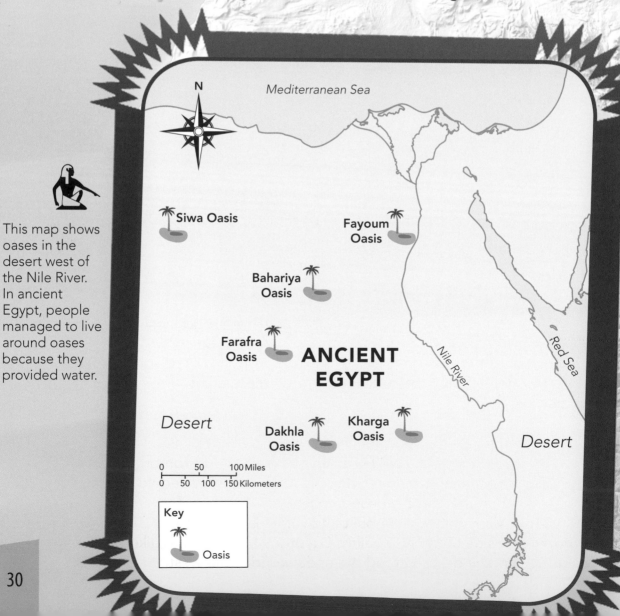

This is the mummy of Ramses II. It has been very well preserved in the hot, dry desert conditions.

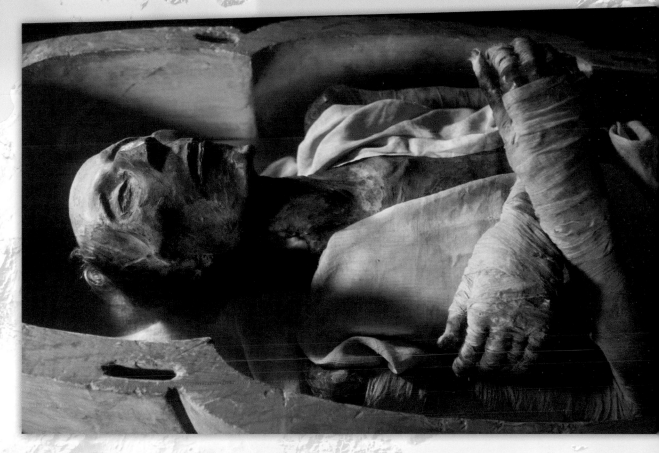

Why were tombs built in dry desert areas?

The hot, dry desert was excellent for preserving dead bodies, so tombs were built in desert areas. Most tombs were built on the desert edges, not too far from the Nile Valley. Egyptians liked having their dead buried close to the living, so these areas were perfect.

To start with, the desert sites were chosen because Egyptians did not want to use up valuable farmland for tombs. Also, tombs built in the valley might have been flooded each year. But people soon realized that the hot, dry desert conditions were best for preservation. Many tombs were built into rocks rising on the western desert side of the Nile Valley. Egyptians believed that, like the setting sun, the dead entered the underworld in the west.

Where Were Ancient Egyptian Towns and Cities?

The earliest settlements along the Nile River were small groups of villages. When Upper Egypt and Lower Egypt united, early kings created a capital city. This was located in the southern part of the Nile Delta and was called Memphis. Many more towns and cities grew up as the civilization grew. Almost all of the settlements were located in the Nile Valley.

How did towns and cities avoid the yearly floods?

The Egyptians built most of their towns and cities close to the Nile River, on the highest land they could find. Since areas of high ground were quite rare, any new buildings were built on the sites of older buildings. Homes in some areas were built to be tall and close together. Some homes rose upward as high as four floor levels. Streets were narrow and crowded.

Were there other capital cities?

The capital city of Egypt was where the land was ruled from. It was never far from the Nile River. The capital city of the Old Kingdom was Memphis. During the Middle Kingdom, the pharaohs moved the capital south to Thebes. Then they moved it to a place called Itj-tawy.

DID YOU KNOW?
The practice of constructing new buildings on top of the ruins of old buildings actually raised the level of the ground over time. This meant that, over the centuries, many towns grew higher above the flood levels.

This is an Egyptian model of a narrow, tall house. It has an open area on the top floor.

During the Hyksos period of rule, their capital was at Avaris, in the Nile Delta. Once they had been defeated and the New Kingdom began, Memphis once more became the capital city. This was until a pharaoh named Akhenaten founded a new capital city, called Akhetaten! In the last few hundred years of ancient Egypt, the capital city was moved to Piramesse, Tanis, Sais, and, finally, Alexandria. These were all in the Nile Delta.

What were ancient Egyptian buildings made of?

Only important buildings such as temples, tombs, and monuments were made of stone. All other buildings were made of mud bricks. People took mud from the riverbanks and mixed it with chopped pieces of straw. They shaped it into bricks and left them to dry in the hot sun.

Houses had thick walls and small windows. This would keep them cool during the hot days and warm during cold nights. Many were whitewashed, to reflect the sun's heat. The small windows also helped to keep out thieves and intruders. Houses near the river, or on lower ground, were sometimes built on raised platforms to guard against flooding.

The village of Deir el-Medina was home to people who built the tombs in the Valley of the Kings near Thebes. Only the stone bases of the buildings remain.

WASTE DISPOSAL

Ancient Egyptian towns and cities had no systems in place for collecting sewage and other waste from buildings. Each household was expected to get rid of its own waste. Some people threw their smelly waste into special waste pits, and others threw it into the Nile River. People who weren't close to waste pits or the river simply threw their waste into the narrow streets!

How did the ancient Egyptians plan their towns?

No mud-brick buildings have survived, because the bricks have crumbled away. However, the stone bases of some towns have survived. Historians have been able to study the layouts of these towns. Many were planned and built far from the Nile Valley for a special purpose, such as building a temple. This means that they were used only temporarily and were not built over like most Egyptian towns.

Boundary walls ran around the town edges. Streets were arranged in grid patterns. Roads had drainage channels running down the middle. Some areas of towns were where important town officials lived and worked. Other areas were for craftworkers and poor laborers.

What Jobs Did Ancient Egyptians Do?

Many Egyptians worked in farming. However, there were many other important jobs in Egyptian society for unskilled workers, highly skilled craftspeople, and educated scholars.

What jobs did unskilled workers do?

People made important everyday items like bread, beer, linen, and mud bricks. To make bread, people ground grain between heavy stones to make flour. They mixed the flour with water to form a dough and baked this in ovens. Beer was made from barley mashed into water and left for a few days.

Other unskilled people worked as servants or as quarry workers. People were not paid money. Instead, they were paid with goods such as food or cloth.

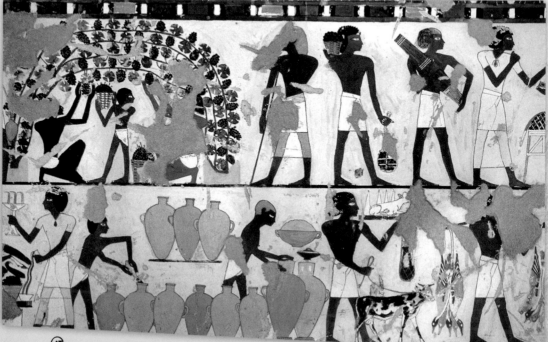

This wall painting shows ancient Egyptians making wine from grapes. You can see workers picking grapes and pouring wine into jars.

DID YOU KNOW?
Some Egyptians had slaves. This was not common in much of Egypt, though, and slavery only really appeared in the New Kingdom. Slaves were usually people captured during periods of war.

Could ancient Egyptians get an education?

There were schools in ancient Egypt, but people had to pay to attend them. Many people couldn't afford this. Most students were boys, but girls from some rich families went to school, too. Students learned to read and write **hieroglyphs**. A boy who could write could become a scribe, an important job in Egypt. Others could go on to study history, literature, religion, geography, languages, surveying, engineering, astronomy, medicine, and accounting.

These are hieroglyphs carved into stone. Each symbol has a different meaning.

What jobs did educated people do?

Very few ancient Egyptian people could read and write hieroglyphs. Scribes were experts at this and were highly respected, wealthy, and important members of Egyptian society. Scribes were employed to take records of all aspects of Egyptian life, including weighing and recording goods like gold and silver.

There were other jobs that educated Egyptians could do. Some were map-makers and made maps of places and also of the stars in the sky. Others were **architects**, designing the amazing pyramids, temples, and tombs. Dentists, doctors, priests, and officials were also highly educated.

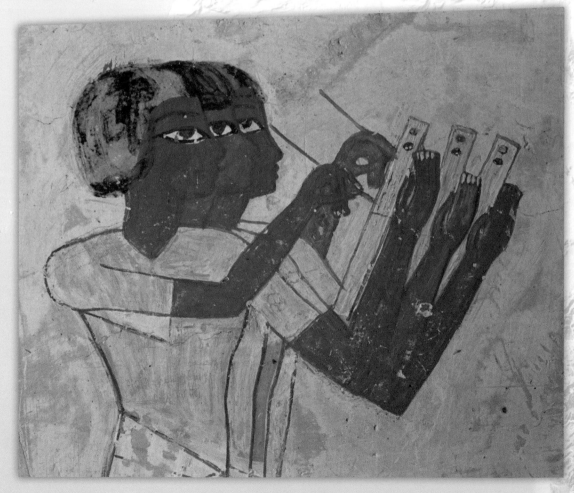

This wall painting shows scribes recording crops being harvested.

This carpenter is shown working on scaffolding using a pick-like tool called an *adze*. It had a copper or bronze blade attached to a wooden handle.

What jobs did skilled workers do?

There were many different skilled workers in Egypt. There were artists who were employed to paint the tombs and temples. They used colored **pigments** to do this. There were carpenters who created furniture, boats, and chariots; metalsmiths and jewelers who made beautiful jewelry; stonemasons who carved statues; potters who made ceramic goods; and glassworkers who made rare glass items. All of these skilled workers made use of the natural resources that Egypt had.

DID YOU KNOW?

Some jobs existed in ancient Egypt that would seem very odd today. In local markets, officials were employed to walk around with "sniffer baboons"! These fierce animals were trained to sniff out goods and catch thieves.

Was Geography Important in Ancient Egyptian Society?

Geography played a huge part in the growth of the ancient Egyptian empire. The shape of the kingdom was created by the course of the Nile River and the coastlines and deserts that formed the kingdom's boundaries. The isolated location of Egypt allowed Egyptian society and culture to develop for thousands of years without interference or influence from other cultures.

In the 1960s, teams of archaeologists carefully moved some Egyptian statues that were in danger of being flooded after the building of the Aswan Dam.

We know a lot about the Egyptians because of all the tombs and temples that were built in the hot, dry desert areas. The climate in these areas means that remains could be preserved for thousands of years.

The climate was important because the yearly floods of the Nile River were crucial to Egyptian life. They kept the land good for farming, and this provided Egyptians with their food. The floods also affected where people could live and how buildings were made.

Lots of people today enjoy visiting buildings and monuments that the ancient Egyptians built.

The natural resources of the Egyptian land played a part in the types of buildings that towns and cities were built from and enabled them to build great tombs, temples, and monuments. The resources also affected people's diets and the goods that could be traded with other countries.

Trade with other countries was affected by transportation links across seas and deserts. Oases provided much-needed water along desert trade routes, and timber imported from other countries was used to build ships to sail on the Mediterranean Sea and Red Sea. Goods were exchanged for other items, rather than for money. All these goods traveled through Egypt along the Nile River.

Quiz

1

How long did the civilization of ancient Egypt last?

a) Around 1,000 years

b) Around 2,000 years

c) Around 3,000 years

2

How many African countries today are in the Nile Basin?

a) Four

b) Ten

c) Nineteen

3

Which continent was ancient Egypt in?

a) Africa

b) North America

c) Asia

4

How much of ancient Egypt was desert?

a) Around 70%

b) Around 80%

c) Around 90%

5

Where does most of the water in the Nile River come from?

a) Huge storms over Egypt

b) Melting glaciers from areas south of Egypt

c) Rain and melting snow from areas south of Egypt

6

Which is the longest river in the world?

a) The Nile

b) The Amazon

c) The Yangtze

7

How did the Egyptians move water from the Nile to their fields?

a) Using a shaduf

b) Using a Nilometer

c) Using papyrus reeds

8

How often did the Nile usually flood?

a) Once a month

b) Once a year

c) Once every two years

9

Where are there many tombs for Egyptian pharaohs?

a) Siwa Oasis

b) The Nile Delta

c) The Valley of the Kings

10

Why were tombs built in desert areas?

a) The hot, dry conditions were best for preserving remains

b) Most people lived in the desert and wanted to be near the tombs

c) The soil was fertile and the tombs could sit in lush gardens

11

Which sea lies to the east of Egypt?

a) The Mediterranean Sea

b) The Black Sea

c) The Red Sea

12

Which animals did Egyptians use at markets to sniff out goods?

a) Dogs

b) Baboons

c) Pigs

Glossary

archaeologist person who studies objects from history to understand past lives

architect person who designs buildings

barren not able to produce or support living things

BCE short for "Before the Common Era," relating to dates before the birth of Jesus Christ

cataract place on a river where the water falls down a waterfall or through narrow, rocky rapids

civilization society that has reached a high level of organization and culture

continent one of Earth's seven large areas of land

culture language, ideas, inventions, traditions, and art of a group of people

delta fan-shaped area at the mouth of a river, created by silt dropped by the river water

embankment mound of earth or stone alongside a river, made to protect the area behind it from flooding

empire group of countries or people ruled over by a powerful leader or government

export take to another country, usually to be sold

famine time when there is not enough food to feed all the people living in an area

fertile able to produce and support plants such as farm crops

hieroglyph picture or symbol that represents something

import bring in from another country, usually to be sold

irrigation system of taking water to crops

mineral substance in Earth that does not come from an animal or a plant

mummy dead body that is preserved with special chemicals and wrapped in cloth or dried out

obelisk tall, thin stone tower with four sides and a pyramid shape at the top

papyrus   tall plant with strong stems, used to make papyrus reeds and paper; papyrus is also the name given to the paper made from papyrus stems

peninsula   piece of land surrounded on nearly all sides by water, and connected to a larger area of land by a usually narrow strip of land

pharaoh   king and ruler in ancient Egypt

pigment   substance that is used to provide color

preserve   keep something in its original condition

rapids   steep section of a river, sometime with rocks in the river channel, where the water flow is fast and turbulent

reservoir   place where water is collected and stored

scribe   person whose job is to write things down, and sometimes make copies of things already written down

scroll   roll of paper, papyrus, or parchment, used for writing and drawing on

settlement   area where people built places to live

shaduf   device for lifting water from one place to another

silt   fine particles of earth, clay, or sand that can be carried by a river, and eventually drop out of the water, usually when the flow is very slow

source   point where a river starts, farthest from the river's mouth

survey   measure

tomb   building that holds the body of a dead person or the bodies of dead people

Find Out More

Books

Brownlie Bojang, Ali. *Egypt in Our World* (Countries in Our World). Mankato, Minn.: Smart Apple Media, 2012.

Catel, Patrick. *What Did the Ancient Egyptians Do for Me?* (Linking the Past and Present). Chicago: Heinemann Library, 2011.

Hart, George. *Ancient Egypt* (Eyewitness). New York City: Dorling Kindersley, 2014.

Rockwood, Leigh. *Ancient Egyptian Geography* (Spotlight on Ancient Civilizations). New York City: PowerKids, 2014.

Web Sites

FactHound offers a safe, fun way to find Internet sites related to this book. All of the sites on FactHound have been researched by our staff.

Here's all you do:

Visit www.facthound.com

Type in this code: 9781484609620

Places to Visit

Carnegie Museum of Natural History, Pittsburgh, Pennsylvania
www.carnegiemnh.org
This museum has the Walton Hall of Ancient Egypt, which features many objects and interactive displays relating to ancient Egypt.

The Metropolitan Museum of Art, New York
www.metmuseum.org
There are lots of different objects from ancient Egypt in this museum's collection.

Tips For Further Research

Nile dams
Today, there are dams across the Nile River. These have been built for many reasons, including to provide hydroelectric power. Do some research into the dams on the Nile River. When was the first one built? Why was it built? How many are there? You could choose one of the dams and create a fact file about it.

The source of the Nile
For many years, people have argued over the exact source of the Nile River—the place where it starts flowing, farthest from its mouth at the Nile Delta. See if you can find out where the agreed upon source of the Nile is, and when this was discovered. How far is it from Egypt?

Index